COME & DRINK

A Daily Devotional for the *Come Thirsty*
Church Experience

MAX LUCADO

NELSON REFERENCE & ELECTRONIC
A Division of Thomas Nelson Publishers
Since 1798

www.thomasnelson.com

Come & Drink by Max Lucado

Copyright © 2004 by Max Lucado

Published in Nashville, Tennessee, by Thomas Nelson Inc.

Excerpts taken from *Grace for the Moment* by Max Lucado, published by J. Countryman, a division of Thomas Nelson Inc. Publishers, copyright © 2000.

Unless otherwise indicated, all Scripture quotations in this book are from the New Century Version (NCV) ©1987, 1988, 1991 by W Publishing Group, Nashville, Tennessee 37214. Used by permission.

Other Scripture references are from the following sources:

The New American Standard Bible (NASB) © 1960, 1962, 1963, 1971, 1972, 1973, 1975, and 1977 by the Lockman Foundation, and are used by permission.

The New International Version of the Bible (NIV) © 1984 by the International Bible Society. Used by permission of Zondervan Bible Publishers.

Library of Congress Cataloging-in-Publication Data Available

ISBN 1-4185-0121-2

Printed in the United States of America

1 2 3 4 5 — 08 07 06 05 04

Clothes of Righteousness

*This body that dies must clothe itself
with something that can never die.*

1 Corinthians 15:53 NCV

Does Jesus care what clothes we wear?

Apparently so. In fact, the Bible tells us exactly the wardrobe God desires.

"But clothe yourselves with the Lord Jesus Christ and forget about satisfying your sinful self" (Rom. 13:14).

"You were all baptized into Christ, and so you were all clothed with Christ. This means that you are all children of God through faith in Christ Jesus" (Gal. 3:26, 27).

This clothing has nothing to do with dresses and jeans and suits. God's concern is with our spiritual garment. He offers a heavenly robe that only heaven can see and only heaven can give. Listen to the words of Isaiah: "The LORD makes me very happy; all that I am rejoices in my God. He has covered me with clothes of salvation and wrapped me with a coat of goodness"(Is. 61:10).

When Christ Comes

DAY 2

A Cut Above

Be still, and know that I am God.

Psalm 46:10 NIV

The word *holy* means "to separate." The ancestry of the term can be traced back to an ancient word which means "to cut." To be holy, then, is to be a cut above the norm, superior, extraordinary…. The Holy One dwells on a different level from the rest of us. What frightens us does not frighten him. What troubles us does not trouble him.

I'm more a landlubber than a sailor, but I've puttered around in a bass boat enough to know the secret for finding land in a storm … You don't aim at another boat. You certainly don't stare at the waves. You set your sights on an object unaffected by the wind—a light on the shore—and go straight toward it….

When you set your sights on our God, you focus on one "a cut above" any storm life may bring…. You find peace.

The Great House of God

Live a Holy Life

You should be a light for other people.
Live so that they will see the good things you do
and will praise your Father in heaven.

Matthew 5:16 NCV

You want to make a difference in your world?
    Live a holy life:
Be faithful to your spouse.
Be the one at the office who refuses to cheat.
Be the neighbor who acts neighborly.
Be the employee who does the work and doesn't
    complain.
Pay your bills.
Do your part and enjoy life.
Don't speak one message and live another.

These aren't merely rules and regulations. They are
simply natural outpourings of God's righteousness in us.
Find ways to demonstrate his righteousness today.
Receive all that he has for you.

A Gentle Thunder

DAY 4

Freedom from Sin

*Now you are free from sin and have
become slaves of God. This brings you a life that
is only for God, and this gives you life forever.*

Romans 6:22 NCV

How could we who have been freed from sin return
to it? Before Christ our lives were out of control, sloppy,
and indulgent. We didn't even know we were slobs until
we met him.

Then he moved in. Things began to change. What we
threw around we began putting away. What we neglected
we cleaned up. What had been clutter became order. Oh,
there were and still are occasional lapses of thought and
deed, but by and large he got our house in order.

Suddenly we find ourselves wanting to do good. Go
back to the old mess? Are you kidding? "In the past you
were slaves to sin—sin controlled you. But thank God,
you fully obeyed the things that you were taught. You
were made free from sin, and now you are slaves to
goodness" (Rom. 6:17, 18).

In the Grip of Grace

God Is Working in You

*Everyone who is a child of God conquers
the world. And this is the victory that
conquers the world—our faith.*

1 John 5:4 NCV

You get impatient with your own life, trying to
master a habit or control a sin—and in your frustration
you begin to wonder where the power of God is. Be
patient. God is using today's difficulties to strengthen
you for tomorrow. He is *equipping* you. The God who
makes things grow will help you bear fruit.

Dwell on the fact that God lives within you. Think
about the power that gives you life. The realization that
God is dwelling within you may change the places you
want to go and the things you want to do today.

Do what is right this week, whatever it is, whatever
comes down the path, whatever problems and dilemmas
you face—just do what's right. Maybe no one else is
doing what's right, but you do what's right. You be
honest. You take a stand. You be true. After all,

regardless of what you do, God does what is right: he saves you with his grace.

Walking with the Savior

DAY 6

Jesus Gives You Victory

*I will forgive their wickedness
and will remember their sins no more.*

Hebrews 8:12 NIV

"Therefore, there is now no condemnation for those
who are in Christ Jesus" (Rom. 8:1 NIV).

"[God] justifies those who have faith in Jesus" (Rom.
3:26 NIV).

For those in Christ, these promises are not only
a source of joy. They are also the foundations of true
courage. You are guaranteed that your sins will be
filtered through, hidden in, and screened out by the
sacrifice of Jesus. When God looks at you, he doesn't
see you; he sees the One who surrounds you. That
means that failure is not a concern for you. Your victory
is secure. How could you not be courageous?

The Applause of Heaven

DAY 7

Adopted by God

*The Spirit himself bears witness with
our Spirit that we are children of God.*

Romans 8:16 NASB

When we come to Christ, God not only forgives
us, he also adopts us. Through a dramatic series of
events, we go from condemned orphans with no hope
to adopted children with no fear. Here is how it happens.
You come before the judgment seat of God full of
rebellion and mistakes. Because of his justice he cannot
dismiss your sin, but because of his love he cannot
dismiss you. So, in an act which stunned the heavens, he
punished himself on the cross for your sins. God's justice
and love are equally honored. And you, God's creation,
are forgiven. But the story doesn't end with God's
forgiveness....

It would be enough if God just cleansed your name,
but he does more. He gives you *his* name.

The Great House of God

God Always Gives Grace

God can do all things.

Mark 10:27 NCV

Our questions betray our lack of understanding:

How can God be everywhere at one time? (Who says God is bound by a body?)

How can God hear all the prayers which come to him? (Perhaps his ears are different from yours.)

How can God be the Father, the Son, and the Holy Spirit? (Could it be that heaven has a different set of physics than earth?)

If people down here won't forgive me, how much more am I guilty before a holy God? (Oh, just the opposite. God is always able to give grace when we humans can't—he invented it.)

The Great House of God

DAY 9

The Basin of God's Grace

The blood of Jesus, God's Son,
cleanses us from every sin.

1 John 1:7 NCV

John tells us, "We are *being cleansed* from every sin by the blood of Jesus." In other words, we are *always being cleansed*. The cleansing is not a promise for the future but a reality in the present. Let a speck of dust fall on the soul of a saint, and it is washed away. Let a spot of filth land on the heart of God's child, and the filth is wiped away....

Our Savior kneels down and gazes upon the darkest acts of our lives. But rather than recoil in horror, he reaches out in kindness and says, "I can clean that if you want." And from the basin of his grace, he scoops a palm full of mercy and washes away our sin.

But that's not all he does. Because he lives in us, you and I can do the same. Because he has forgiven us, we can forgive others.

Just Like Jesus

From Heaven Itself

God made you alive with Christ,
and he forgave all your sins. He canceled the debt,
which listed all the rules we failed to follow.

Colossians 2:13, 14 NCV

All the world religions can be placed in one of two camps: legalism or grace. Humankind does it or God does it. Salvation as a wage based on deeds done—or salvation as a gift based on Christ's death.

A legalist believes the supreme force behind salvation is you. If you look right, speak right, and belong to the right segment of the right group, you will be saved. The brunt of responsibility doesn't lie within God; it lies within you.

The result? The outside sparkles. The talk is good and the step is true. But look closely. Listen carefully. Something is missing. What is it? Joy. What's there? Fear. (That you won't do enough.) Arrogance. (That you have done enough.) Failure. (That you have made a mistake.)

Spiritual life is not a human endeavor. It is rooted in and orchestrated by the Holy Spirit. Every spiritual achievement is created and energized by God.

He Still Moves Stones

God Listens

I cry out to the LORD;
I pray to the LORD for mercy.

Psalm 142:1 NCV

You can talk to God because God listens. Your voice
matters in heaven. He takes you very seriously. When
you enter his presence, he turns to you to hear your
voice. No need to fear that you will be ignored. Even if
you stammer or stumble, even if what you have to say
impresses no one, it impresses God, and he listens. He
listens to the painful plea of the elderly in the rest home.
He listens to the gruff confession of the death-row
inmate. When the alcoholic begs for mercy, when the
spouse seeks guidance, when the businessman steps off
the street into the chapel, God listens.

Intently. Carefully.

The Great House of God

DAY 12

See What God Has Done!

The heavens tell the glory of God.

Psalm 19:1 NCV

How vital that we pray, armed with the knowledge that God is in heaven. Pray with any lesser conviction and your prayers are timid, shallow, and hollow. But spend some time walking in the workshop of the heavens, seeing what God has done, and watch how your prayers are energized....

Behold the sun! Every square yard of the sun is constantly emitting 130,000 horse power, or the equivalent of 450 eight-cylinder automobile engines. And yet our sun, as powerful as it is, is but one minor star in the 100 billion orbs which make up our Milky Way Galaxy. Hold a dime in your fingers and extend it arm's length toward the sky, allowing it to eclipse your vision, and you will block out fifteen million stars from your view.... By showing us the heavens, Jesus is showing us his Father's workshop.... He taps us on the shoulder and says, "Your Father can handle that for you."

The Great House of God

Prayers Make a Difference

We all know that God does not listen to sinners, but he listens to anyone who worships and obeys him.

John 9:31 NCV

Most of our prayer lives could use a tune-up.

Some prayer lives lack consistency. They're either a desert or an oasis. Long, arid, dry spells interrupted by brief plunges into the waters of communion....

Others of us need sincerity. Our prayers are a bit hollow, memorized, and rigid. More liturgy than life. And though they are daily, they are dull.

Still others lack, well, honesty. We honestly wonder if prayer makes a difference. Why on earth would God in heaven want to talk to me? If God knows all, who am I to tell him anything? If God controls all, who am I to do anything?

Our prayers may be awkward. Our attempts may be feeble. But since the power of prayer is in the One who hears it and not the one who says it, our prayers do make a difference.

He Still Moves Stones

DAY 14

Boldness Before the Throne

*Let us, then, feel very sure that we can
come before God's throne where there is grace.*

Hebrews 4:16 NCV

Jesus tells us … ,"When you pray, pray like this. 'Our Father who is in heaven, hallowed be thy name. Thy kingdom come.'"

When you say, "Thy kingdom come," you are inviting the Messiah himself to walk into your world. "Come, my King! Take your throne in our land. Be present in my heart. Be present in my office. Come into my marriage. Be Lord of my family, my fears, and my doubts." This is no feeble request; it's a bold appeal for God to occupy every corner of your life.

[And] who are you to ask such a thing? Who are you to ask God to take control of your world? You are his child, for heaven's sake! And so you ask boldly.

The Great House of God

God Hears Our Prayers

The LORD hears good people when
they cry out to him, and he saves them
from all their troubles.

Psalm 34:17 NCV

When [a friend] told Jesus of the illness [of Lazarus] he said, "Lord, the one you love is sick." He doesn't base his appeal on the imperfect love of the one in need, but on the perfect love of the Savior. He doesn't say, "The one *who loves you* is sick." He says, "The one *you love* is sick." The power of the prayer, in other words, does not depend on the one who makes the prayer, but on the One who hears the prayer.

We can and must repeat the phrase in manifold ways. "The one you love is tired, sad, hungry, lonely, fearful, depressed." The words of the prayer vary, but the response never changes. The Savior hears the prayer. He silences heaven, so he won't miss a word. He hears the prayer.

The Great House of God

DAY 16

Worthless Worry

I was young, and now I am old,
but I have never seen good people left helpless
or their children begging for food.

Psalm 37:25 NCV

We worry. We worry about the IRS and the SAT and the FBI.... We worry that we won't have enough money, and when we have money we worry that we won't manage it well. We worry that the world will end before the parking meter expires. We worry what the dog thinks if he sees us step out of the shower. We worry that someday we'll learn that fat-free yogurt was fattening.

Honestly, now. Did God save you so you would fret? Would he teach you to walk just to watch you fall? Would he be nailed to the cross for your sins and then disregard your prayers? Come on. Is Scripture teasing us when it reads, "He has put his angels in charge of you to watch over you wherever you go"? (Ps. 91:11).

I don't think so either.

In the Grip of Grace

A Heart Like His

We are like clay, and you are the potter;
your hands made us all.

Isaiah 64:8 NCV

[God] wants us to be just like Jesus.

Isn't that good news? You aren't stuck with today's personality. You aren't condemned to "grumpydom." You are tweakable. Even if you've worried each day of your life, you needn't worry the rest of your life. So what if you were born a bigot? You don't have to die one.

Where did we get the idea we can't change? From whence come statements such as, "It's just my nature to worry" or, "I'll always be pessimistic. I'm just that way." … Who says? Would we make similar statements about our bodies? "It's just my nature to have a broken leg. I can't do anything about it." Of course not. If our bodies malfunction, we seek help. Shouldn't we do the same with our hearts? Shouldn't we seek aid for our sour attitudes? Can't we request treatment for our selfish tirades? Of course we can. Jesus can change our hearts. He wants us to have a heart like his.

Just Like Jesus

DAY 18

God Cares About You

Look at the birds in the air.
They don't plant or harvest or store food in
barns, but your heavenly Father feeds them.

Matthew 6:26 NCV

Consider the earth! Our globe's weight has been estimated at six sextillion tons (a six with twenty-one zeroes). Yet it is precisely tilted at twenty-three degrees; any more or any less and our seasons would be lost in a melted polar flood. Though our globe revolves at the rate of one-thousand miles per hour or twenty-five thousand miles per day or nine million miles per year, none of us tumbles into orbit....

As you stand ... observing God's workshop, let me pose a few questions. If he is able to place the stars in their sockets and suspend the sky like a curtain, do you think it is remotely possible that God is able to guide your life? If your God is mighty enough to ignite the sun, could it be that he is mighty enough to light your path? If he cares enough about the planet Saturn to give it rings or Venus to make it sparkle, is there an outside chance that he cares enough about you to meet your needs?

The Great House of God

DAY 19

God's Will . . . Be Done

*May your kingdom come
and what you want be done,
here on earth as it is in heaven.*

Matthew 6:10 NCV

To pray, "Thy will be done" is to seek the heart of God. The word *will* means "strong desire." ... [So] what is his heart? His passion? He wants you to know it.

Shall God hide from us what he is going to do? Apparently not, for he has gone to great lengths to reveal his will to us. Could he have done more than send his Son to lead us? Could he have done more than give his word to teach us? Could he have done more than orchestrate events to awaken us? Could he have done more than send his Holy Spirit to counsel us?

God is not the God of confusion, and wherever he sees sincere seekers with confused hearts, you can bet your sweet December that he will do whatever it takes to help them see his will.

The Great House of God

Day 20

God's Priority

*Depend on the LORD; trust him,
and he will take care of you.*

Psalm 37:5 NCV

God is committed to caring for our needs. Paul tells us that a man who won't feed his own family is worse than an unbeliever (1 Tim. 5:8). How much more will a holy God care for his children? After all, how can we fulfill his mission unless our needs are met? How can we teach or minister or influence unless we have our basic needs satisfied? Will God enlist us in his army and not provide a commissary? Of course not.

"I pray that the God of peace will give you everything you need so you can do what he wants" (Heb. 13:20). Hasn't that prayer been answered in our life? We may not have had a feast, but haven't we always had food? Perhaps there was no banquet, but at least there was bread. And many times there *was* a banquet.

The Great House of God

DAY 21

Just the Way You Are

In your lives you must
think and act like Christ Jesus.

Philippians 2:5 NCV

It's dangerous to sum up grand truths in one state-
ment, but I'm going to try. If a sentence or two could
capture God's desire for each of us, it might read like
this:

God loves you just the way you are, but he refuses
to leave you that way. He wants you to be just like Jesus.

God loves you just the way you are. If you think his
love for you would be stronger if your faith were, you are
wrong. If you think his love would be deeper if your
thoughts were, wrong again. Don't confuse God's love
with the love of people. The love of people often
increases with performance and decreases with mistakes.
Not so with God's love. He loves you right where you
are.

Just Like Jesus

DAY 22

You're Something Special

*Nothing ... in the whole world will ever
be able to separate us from the love of God.*

Romans 8:39 NCV

We want to know how long God's love will
endure.... Not just on Easter Sunday when our shoes are
shined and our hair is fixed.... Not when I'm peppy and
positive and ready to tackle world hunger. Not then. I
know how he feels about me then. Even I like me then.

I want to know how he feels about me when I snap
at anything that moves, when my thoughts are gutter-
level, when my tongue is sharp enough to slice a rock.
How does he feel about me then?

Can anything separate us from the love Christ has
for us?

God answered our question before we asked it. So
we'd see his answer, he lit the sky with a star. So we'd
hear it, he filled the night with a choir; and so we'd
believe it, he did what no man had ever dreamed. He
became flesh and dwelt among us.

He placed his hand on the shoulder of humanity and said, "You're something special."

In the Grip of Grace

Jesus Understands

He took our suffering on him
and felt our pain for us.

Isaiah 53:4 NCV

Jesus knows how you feel. You're under the gun at work? Jesus knows how you feel. You've got more to do than is humanly possible? So did he. People take more from you than they give? Jesus understands. Your teenagers won't listen? Your students won't try? Jesus knows how you feel.

You are precious to him. So precious that he became like you so that you would come to him.

When you struggle, he listens. When you yearn, he responds. When you question, he hears. He has been there.

In the Eye of the Storm

DAY 24

Removing Doubt

*Who is more important: the one
sitting at the table or the one serving?
You think the one at the table is more important,
but I am like a servant among you.*

Luke 22:27 NCV

In Jesus' day the washing of feet was a task reserved not just for servants but for the lowest of servants. Every circle has its pecking order, and the circle of household workers was no exception. The servant at the bottom of the totem pole was expected to be the one on his knees with the towel and basin.

In this case the one with the towel and basin is the King of the universe. Hands that shaped the stars now wash away filth. Fingers that formed mountains now massage toes. And the One before whom all nations will one day kneel now kneels before his disciples. Hours before his own death, Jesus' concern is singular. He wants his disciples to know how much he loves them. More than removing dirt, Jesus is removing doubt.

Just Like Jesus

God Is Crazy About You

*God even knows how
many hairs are on your head.*

Matthew 10:30 NCV

There are many reasons God saves you: to bring glory to himself, to appease his justice, to demonstrate his sovereignty. But one of the sweetest reasons God saved you is because he is fond of you. He likes having you around. He thinks you are the best thing to come down the pike in quite a while.…

If God had a refrigerator, your picture would be on it. If he had a wallet, your photo would be in it. He sends you flowers every spring and a sunrise every morning. Whenever you want to talk, he'll listen. He can live anywhere in the universe, and he chose your heart.…

Face it, friend. He's crazy about you.

A Gentle Thunder